A Brief History of

Standards

in Teacher Education

Roy A. Edelfelt and James D. Raths

Association of Teacher Educators

Association of Teacher Educators
1900 Association Drive, Suite ATE
Reston, VA 20191-1502

Roy A. Edelfelt is a clinical professor at The University of North Carolina at Chapel Hill.
James D. Raths is a professor at the University of Delaware.

An earlier version of this monograph was created for the National Academy on the Alignment of Standards and Teacher Development for Student Learning, held in June 1998 and cosponsored by ATE, the American Association of Colleges for Teacher Education, and the National Council for Accreditation of Teacher Education.

Cover design by Daniel Soileau, Chapel Hill, North Carolina
Text design and editing by Edelfelt Johnson, Chapel Hill, North Carolina

Contents

ALMOST FROM THE BEGINNING of formal teacher education, teacher educators have been concerned about standards for their programs and candidates. In 1869, at the Fifth Annual Meeting of the American Normal School Association, the organization's first vice president advanced the following motion for consideration:

> Whereas, The elements of our professional science exist in a chaotic state, and, whereas, we believe the cause of education would be materially benefited by having these elements systematically arranged that there might be uniformity in all the Normal Schools, both in theory and practice. Therefore,
>
> Resolved, That there be appointed by the Association an Educational Council, or Committee, whose duty it shall be to report at our next annual meeting on the following, viz., 1. What properly constitutes the "Science of Education," as applicable to the Normal Schools and the teaching profession generally? 2. What "Course of Study and Practice" in the Normal School is best calculated to elevate the standard of education and to reduce teaching to a uniform system and regular profession?
>
> Resolved, That the Committee report through the educational journals of the country previous to the next meeting of the Association. (pp. 34–35)

(How the motion fared is not clear. The minutes make no further reference to it.)

The concerns and the assumptions reflected in this motion made 130 years ago are similar to those in recent reports and recommendations. First, there is an assumption that, from the disarray of scientific findings and practical experiences, teacher educators can develop a code that will define "best practice." Second, discomfort with diverse practices is evident: Some approaches to teaching and teacher education must be better than others. Through a standard-setting process, the profession should identify and encourage the better practices and eradicate the weaker ones. In short, the motion calls for alignment.

In 1870 a proposal advanced at the Sixth Annual Meeting of the American Normal School Association spelled out criteria for admission to teacher education programs and a two-year course of study for normal schools. Phrasing standards in terms of "weeks of instruction," the criteria included topics such as "ethical instruction" and "the theory and practice of instruction." The proposed criteria were met with fierce objection.

Another aspect of standard setting in the 1870s that mirrored current applications of accreditation standards was the notion of "context." In the language of the 1870 proposal,

> The normal school is compelled by necessities of its position in the system, to adjust itself to the circumstances of the subordinate parts of that system. It must at first let itself down so far as possible to be accessible by average of those who have received their preparation in the lower schools. Otherwise, its rooms would be tenantless and its occupation would be gone. (American Normal School Association, 1870, p. 18)

Even then, there was an awareness that standards must be reality based.

In the early 1870s, after the American Normal School Association became the Department of Normal Schools of the National Education Association (NEA), it petitioned the then-fledgling regional associations (North Central, Middle States, etc.) for accreditation of its programs. Evidently those groups rebuffed teacher education as not worthy of such efforts (Haberman & Stinnett, 1973; Mayor, 1965).

As late as 1899, a report to the Department of Normal Schools by a committee appointed four years previously, set standards for almost all phases of teacher education. Running more than 40 pages, the report made recommendations that were broad in scope and specific in language. For example (NEA, Department of Normal Schools, 1899):

> Admission: The applicant shall have finished a grammar-school course embracing the following subjects, in which he is reasonably proficient: arithmetic, English grammar, geography, United States history, physiology and hygiene, drawing, civil government, music, grammar-school algebra, nature study, reading, penmanship, spelling, and English. (p. 843)
>
> Clinical Experiences: The number of children entrusted to a beginning student teacher should be small, approximately ten or twelve. (p. 846)
>
> Administration: The training school should be practically under the control of the normal-school authorities to such an extent that the latter can formulate a curriculum, select text-books, choose and dismiss teachers, determine methods, and in general administer the affairs of the school according to their own best judgment. (pp. 846–47)

Up to that time, efforts in the 19th century to advance standards had had little effect. There were no procedures for closing down programs and institutions deemed to be substandard. Then, as now, teacher education was a cottage industry.

A Definition of Standards

Some current advocates of standards in teacher education have taken time in their writings to ask, "What are standards?" Both Richardson (1994) and Pearson (1994) eventually turned to the dictionary for definitions, rather than to the technical literature on evaluation and measurement. Richardson advanced the following notions (p. 16):

1. Something that is established by authority, custom, or general consent as a model or example to be followed.
2. A definite level of degree of quality that is proper or adequate for a specific purpose.

Pearson cited the same definition (probably because he had referred to the same dictionary) but also offered synonyms, including "criterion," "gauge," "yardstick," "touchstone," and "test" (p. 38).

In a seminal essay, Glass (1978) described the ways in which many evaluators looked at the concept of standards. He pointed out in effect that evaluators had been using the term "standards" incorrectly. According to Glass, "criterion" is a variable of concern in making a decision, "standard" the "amount" of the variable that is needed to meet the criterion. So, for example, a criterion for becoming a police officer in Champaign, Illinois, is height. The standard is 5 feet.

Current and previous rhetoric does not recognize the Glass distinction. Instead, "standard" is used as a synonym for "criterion."

A pervasive problem in the professions is people operating with criteria and no standards. So universities promote, or deny promotion to, professors on the basis of three criteria: quality of teaching, scholarly productivity, and extent of service. Rarely are those criteria accompanied by standards. Applying the criteria in these situations requires judgment. Reliance on professional judgment is a hallmark of the current procedure of the National Council for Accreditation of Teacher Education (NCATE)—its strength and its weakness. Recognizing that strict standards either could not be set or would not be accepted, NCATE dropped strict standards, for the most part, and invoked the judgments of members of its Board of Examiners in making decisions about particular cases. The problem is that members' judgments vary across institutions and occasions, and this has prompted serious challenges to the credibility of NCATE decisions.

This discussion of criteria and standards is relevant to current concerns with setting standards in teacher education and to the competency-based teacher education movement of 1970 or so. How are today's standards different from the behavioral objectives of that earlier day? Later in this paper we discuss issues associated with competency-based teacher education.

Examples of Standard-Setting Efforts

In the last two centuries, there have been innumerable studies of and declarations on standards in teacher education—efforts to identify criteria for teacher preparation institutions, teacher education curricula, prospective teachers, beginning teachers, practicing teachers, teachers in various disciplines, and teacher educators. In the following section, we describe some representative ones. We do not include current undertakings, such as those of the Interstate New Teacher Assessment and Support Consortium (INTASC) or the National Commission on Teaching & America's Future. At the end of this book, we present a partial bibliography of other reports.

The Commonwealth Teacher-Training Study, 1929

In the 1920s, studies dealing with education for the professions entered a new stage, that of critical analysis. The Carnegie Foundation for the Advancement of Teaching and the Commonwealth Fund were central in sponsoring these investigations. The Commonwealth Teacher-Training Study, a five-year undertaking supported by a $42,000 grant, was responsible for a "new approach to the problems of professional [teacher] education" (Charters & Waples, 1929, p. xv). The aim of the new approach, called "functional studies," was "to determine what the professional practitioner does under modern conditions of practice" (p. xvi). Then, from an objective record of what the practitioner does, the observer attempts to determine what the practitioner must know and be able to do to perform effectively. (Does that sound familiar?) One of the most exhaustive applications of this new method, the Commonwealth Teacher-Training Study was thought to be timely because the preparation of teachers was deemed the most vexing of "all the curriculum problems in higher education" (p. xvi). This was a time when graduation from high school was sufficient for entry into normal school.

Thousands of books and unrecorded experiences were considered potential content for teacher training curricula. All these data made a "substantial contribution to educational theory and practice." Needed was "a basis for selection from this unwieldy mass of information" (p. 3).

Project staff selected the activities and traits of teachers and "useful methods and principles from the accumulation of race [course of life] experience" (p. 4). The activities and traits of excellent teachers of all types, in all kinds and at all levels of schools, including experimental schools, were determined. In a survey, teachers were asked to judge activities on three criteria: importance, difficulty of learning, and value of preservice training. They also were asked to indicate the frequency of use of activities. Superintendents, principals, education professors, supervisors, and other experts were polled to corroborate the teachers' judgments. In exploring ways to put these evaluated activities to practical use, it became necessary to define teacher objectives in order "to select appropriate methods of performing the activities" (p. 5). Recognizing that appropriate methods should be decided on the basis of individual judgments, no attempt was made to "formulate a list of objectives for [all] teacher training institutions" (p. 5). However, objectives were assumed when the authors illustrated the procedures involved in constructing a given curriculum or course. The contention was that, when the constructor of curriculum knew the teachers' activities and objectives, he or she then must explore the problems and the difficulties of both. That made the problems and the difficulties the focus of teacher training. The prospective teacher was then required to select efficient methods for their solution. If the activities were to be recommended and if the prospective teacher was to be taught how to perform them, it was "the function of the teacher training curriculum to provide this information" (p. 6). In moving from activities to methods of teaching, the report cited the importance of principles in the adaptation of materials into a course of study. It also recognized adapting a course to the needs of students as a factor. So, even at this early stage of pedagogical discussion, considering methods, content, and students received extensive attention.

As for traits, the authors admitted to a conundrum: "One must either select teachers who possess the desired traits to begin with or develop the traits in the training school and during the first few years of service" (p. 15). Thus began a decades-long discussion of teacher behavior and performance. Competency-based and outcomes-based teacher education brought new language to very similar concepts. Despite the difference in terminology, the dilemma persists today.

The Improvement of Teacher Education, 1946

In 1938 the American Council on Education created the Commission on Teacher Education. The commission functioned until 1944, devoting itself primarily to experimentation and demonstration in the field and implementation of existing research, rather than to promotion of further inquiry.

Initially the commission intended to include only colleges and universities in its study. However, after its establishment, recognizing the many factors and personnel involved in teacher education, it decided to include school systems and statewide cooperating groups as well. Composed of 16 members, the commission represented all three of these constituencies.

The commission reported its results in eight books. In the final volume (American Council on Education, Commission on Teacher Education, 1946), Karl Bigelow, director of the commission's efforts, wrote,

> The commission] is of the sober opinion that the improvement of teacher education is of the greatest national importance in our times. And it cannot but believe that its own unique experience provides a basis for suggestions and recommendations that are of genuine significance. (p. xx).

The areas studied and demonstrated encompassed the full scope of teacher education as it existed at the time (and as it exists now): personnel services, selection and recruitment, placement and follow-up, curriculum, general education, subject-matter preparation, professional education, student teaching, five-year programs, inservice education for teachers, and preparation and inservice growth of college teachers. Overall, the work of the commission was grounded in a democratic philosophy. The commission was strongly committed to the goal of aligning teaching and teacher education with basic social needs. It strongly emphasized democratic values in its rhetoric and relied heavily on democratic procedures in its recommended actions.

The recommendations of the commission essentially set standards in each of the areas addressed. Most have been pursued in the years since, some successfully, others not.

School and Community Laboratory Experiences in Teacher Education, 1948

In 1945 the Committee on Standards and Surveys of the American Association of Teachers Colleges (AATC; now the American Association of Colleges for Teacher Education, AACTE) appointed a subcommittee to study student teaching in the professional education of teachers. The standards for student teaching had not been revised in about 25 years.

The subcommittee developed a set of principles to work toward qualitative standards and then produced a questionnaire to ascertain current and anticipated practices in the field. It sent the questionnaire to all the member institutions of AATC and to 50 liberal arts colleges where serious and promising programs in teacher education were under way. The intent was to determine the field's readiness for improving standards and to identify the aspects of student teaching to which that readiness might be applied.

In June 1946 a volunteer group of some 40 AATC members met to review the suggested principles, to discuss reactions to the questionnaire, and to point out issues and problems in student teaching. The result was a decision that it was time to apply to professional education what was known about how learning takes place. The group called attention to the dichotomy between theory and practice and concluded that direct experience should be a significant part of professional education. The group established two definitions, one for professional laboratory experience and the other for student teaching.

Another decision at the June meeting was to hold regional conferences to increase participation in the study, help the subcommittee become acquainted firsthand with problems in the field, check the accuracy of interpretations of questionnaire data, and learn more about promising practices.

During the 1946–47 academic year, three conferences took place (in Terre Haute, Indiana; Washington, D.C.; and Minneapolis) to discuss issues of concern. The conferences included representatives from 39 institutions. Margaret Lindsey, a professor at Indiana State Teachers College who had been retained as subcommittee staff, also visited 10 selected colleges to study promising practices in implementing the established principles and to identify problems and barriers in translating principles into action. The subcommittee chose the 10 colleges to gain wide geographic representation, to include various types of institutions, and to involve some colleges that had not participated in the Commission on Teacher Education study (1938–44).

The subcommittee's publication *School and Community Laboratory Experiences in Teacher Education* (Sub-Committee, 1948), known familiarly as the Flowers Report (after John Flowers, chair of the subcommittee), described the standards for laboratory experiences that developed from the subcommittee's efforts. The standards addressed the place of laboratory experiences in the college curriculum, their nature, assignment and length, guidance and supervision, and facilities. Ultimately the standards became Standard VI of the AATC accreditation standards and subsequently part of NCATE standards.

Examples of the subcommittee's recommendations were that (1) laboratory experiences be an integral part of work in each of the four years of college; (2) before student teaching, laboratory experiences be integrated into other parts of the college program; (3) provisions be made for post-student-teaching experiences; (4) provisions be made for full-time student teaching; (5) assignments be made cooperatively by the people most acquainted with the student and his or her needs and the opportunities in the laboratory situation; and (6) the college faculty member and the cooperating teacher share in supervision.

New Horizons for the Teaching Profession, 1961

As the nation was catching its breath after World War II, the teaching profession, represented broadly by leaders in the National Education Association (NEA), accrediting bodies, and higher education, became increasingly aware of the need to take charge of quality issues associated with education. This new awareness prompted the NEA to establish the National Commission on Teacher Education and Professional Standards, known familiarly as the TEPS Commission. The TEPS Commission was charged "with responsibility for carrying on a continuing program for the profession in matters of selection and recruitment, preparation, certification, in-service growth, and the advancement of professional standards" (Lindsey, 1961, p. vii).

In the angst of the postwar years and following the launching of Sputnik in 1957, education leaders perceived the American public as becoming more and more suspicious of the standards held by the teaching profession. There was widespread fear that nonprofessionals would rush in to "take over." This general concern led in 1959 to the Project on New Horizons in Teacher Education and Professional Standards. The TEPS Commission charged project personnel with developing "definitive statements in the areas of responsibility assigned to the National Commission on Teacher Education and Professional Standards that would serve as guides at the local, state, and national levels" (Lindsey, 1961, pp. viii–ix). The project's report, edited by Lindsey (1961), project director and by this time professor of education at Teachers College, Columbia University, covered a wide range of topics. The following paragraphs summarize those most pertinent to teacher education.

The report identified two major players in policy making for teaching and teacher education: the state and the profession. In uncompromising language the report attributed to the first player, the state, the statutory responsibility for certification of teachers and approval of teacher education programs. It defined the second player, the profession, as those who teach in schools; those who teach professional education in colleges and universities; those who work in state departments of education and other government agencies, such as the U.S. Office of Education (predecessor to the U.S. Department of Education); professional personnel in organizations directly related to teaching at any level; and professional personnel in voluntary accrediting agencies. This conception of the profession, which has in many respects carried forward to current times, reduced the voice and the authority of college and university faculty. That may in part explain the slow progress made in implementing the standards advanced by the project.

The project called for reaching a consensus on what represented competent practice: "It is recommended that the National Commission on Teacher Education and Professional Standards, in cooperation with other agencies, establish a comprehensive definition of teacher competence acceptable to the profession" (p. 226). Compared with the current bandying about of "excellence" and "world-class standards," the mild language is of interest. Again the quest reflected a common theme in teacher education's history—seeking a definition of effective practice. The authors did provide a caveat:

> An unrealistic vision of what it is hoped these competencies might become will not suffice, because the profession must be prepared to rise or fall in terms of progress made in requiring every member to attain them. Agreed-upon criteria of competence thus become an expression of serious commitment. (p. 216)

In spite of assigning teacher education and a variety of other groups the role of collaborator, the project recommended that teacher education become a total institutional responsibility. This may have been the birth of the "unit" concept that now dominates NCATE. In some respects the recommendation distanced teacher education from the normal school concept of professional education. Smith (1980) saw this recommendation as a root cause of the intractability of teacher education over time.

Other recommended standards for teacher education included the following (pp. 236–37):

1. Teacher education should be "staffed by fully prepared educators who perform with excellence."
2. Teacher education should be characterized by "broad liberal education."
3. Teacher education should include "an internship, in addition to student teaching and other laboratory experiences, as an integral part of the program."
4. Teacher education should be characterized by "appropriate use of both qualitative and quantitative evaluation of student progress."

The report also urged NCATE to adopt standards that met four conditions (p. 239):

1. [They] are based on continuing study, research, and experimentation.
2. [They] are stated in terms that facilitate understanding of them and appraisal of programs in relation to them.
3. [They] may be viewed as stimulating improvement as well as regulating practice.
4. [They] not only provide for but actually require institutional experimentation with varied approaches to the preparation of professional personnel.

Educating a Profession, 1976

In 1974 the AACTE Board of Directors appointed the Commission on Education for the Profession of Teaching. Members included Robert Howsam, University of Houston, chair; Dean Corrigan, University of Vermont; George Denemark, University of Kentucky; and Robert Nash, University of Vermont. The commission was charged "to examine all aspects of American education and the teaching profession which have relevance for teacher education institutions and the Association, to draft recommendations, and to report in time for the Annual AACTE Meeting of the Bicentennial [1976] year" (Howsam, Corrigan, Denemark, & Nash, 1976, p. 1). The phrase "and the Association" suggested a provincialism that may have accounted for some self-serving recommendations. Most of the recommendations, however, were open-minded and free of organizational bias—probably one of the reasons that AACTE "accepted" the report as opposed to endorsing it.

The first two chapters examined the characteristics of professions and the extent to which teaching (in the mid-1970s) met the criteria for a profession. This analysis provided a set of criteria for judging professions. In chapter 2 the commission made 24 assertions about the teaching profession, advancing forthrightly its positions on the critical issues dealt with in the report.

The remaining three chapters addressed the central parts of the charge, "to examine all aspects of American education" and the teaching profession. Interspersed in these final chapters were 52 recommendations—essentially criteria—for education and teacher education. Most are the familiar ones for improving the essence of teacher education.

The report also gave attention to several topics not often considered in such an examination: the role of governance in teacher education; the lack of autonomy of schools and colleges of education in the university (and their control of only 25 percent of preparation); the "absence of any outside force" (p. 60), notably professional organizations, to support teacher education politically or institutionally; the school or college of education's need to extend formal contact to beginning teachers (with a supervised internship); and the need to expand professional education beyond the school, creating a new kind of teacher, a "human service educator." On the latter subject, the commission suggested that "a number of generic competencies are relevant to all the human service professions" (p. 104). A recommendation for adequate "life space" in the education of teachers (i.e., adequate time and resources to prepare professional teachers) was discussed, as was professional culture. Interestingly these were treated separately from helping neophytes develop humanistic values and attitudes.

Another commission recommendation was the attainment of professional literacy—that is, acquisition of knowledge about important educational and sociopolitical issues and the capability of interacting effectively with concerned citizens in resolving those issues. This notion is not often mentioned in teacher education.

In numerous places in its report, and in various ways, the commission expressed dismay at the current status of teaching as a profession [e.g., "Most teachers have a far from adequate knowledge of presently available principles, practices, and theories" (p. 11)]. At the same time, it viewed teaching as *a matter of life and death* (p. 15), admitting that teachers were "professionals charged with one of the most complex and demanding responsibilities imaginable" (p. 80) and advocating a goal of making teaching a profession.

The commission thought that the education of teacher educators, as of 1976, was "largely ignored in the professional literature," and it addressed that concern in some detail, in a section worthy of examination today (pp. 105–8). Seldom have teacher educators examined themselves. Paralleling that notion were several related ones: the admittedly inferior status of teacher education in higher education, the lack of a knowledge base for teaching, the low self-concept of teachers, and the tendency of teacher educators "who question the importance of their own field [to] begin to seek ways to achieve conventional academic stature" (p. 108).

Unique to this study was a 1985 reprint of the original report with a postscript by the three surviving members of the commission. The postscript assessed progress on the recommendations made in 1976. In doing so, it recognized, as few other studies have done, the difference in factors such as economic climate and teacher supply and demand from the time of the original report to the time of the reprint.

As might be expected, the authors made some additional recommendations. Most relevant to the current scene was a proposal to establish a viable coalition of professional organizations to commission, conduct, and encourage studies of the political, bureaucratic, and other controls and influences on the teaching profession. Related was a recommendation for collaboration in policy making to influence public opinion and public policy.

A Design for a School of Pedagogy, 1980

A Design for a School of Pedagogy, published in 1980, was based in part on the experiences of its author, B. O. Smith, in the National Teacher Corps. Readers need to understand more completely the impact of the National Teacher Corps experience on the thinking of teacher educators who were engaged in it and their subsequent influence on the field.

The report begins with a generous nod to previous efforts to improve teacher education through research and report writing, but it asserts that they shared three flaws: (1) failure to take into account the influence that colleges and universities had on teacher education taking place in the higher education context; (2) insufficient crediting of the knowledge base of teaching; and (3) disregard of the schism between theory and practice and ways that the gap might be closed in teacher preparation programs.

After advancing his proposals for "schools of pedagogy," Smith suggested ways of reaching his goals. He advocated leadership within the universities to bring about the changes he recommended, but he explicitly stated that such leadership would not be sufficient. He advocated application of stronger "external circumstances" to higher education, including accreditation systems, state approval mechanisms, and statewide examinations.

The Power of Competency-Based Teacher Education, 1972

The Power of Competency-Based Teacher Education, issued in 1972 by a quasi-governmental group, the Committee on National Program Priorities in Teacher Education, expressed the views of the competency-based movement at its height. The front matter of the book states that the report was developed under a contract with the U.S. Government but that its "content does not necessarily reflect the position or policy of that Agency" (Rosner, 1972, p. ii). However, the U.S. Office of Education had shown particular interest in competency-based teacher education. During the late 1960s, it had solicited proposals for the redesign of elementary school teacher education programs. A large number of institutions submitted preliminary proposals, and subsequently as many as 20 institutions received funds to refine their original thinking. The competition was limited by the condition that proposals be "competency-based." The report included a number of thoughtful chapters on issues associated with competency-based teacher education, such as exploring local options; linking the movement to a contemporary report from AACTE, *Teachers for the Real World* (Smith, 1969); and building public school–university consortia for teacher education.

The book did not define competency-based teacher education, but Elam (1971) was generally recognized at the time as advancing the most credible definition. According to him, competency-based teacher education had to include the following elements (p. 67):

1. Competencies (knowledge skills, behaviors) to be demonstrated by the student are derived from explicit conceptions of teacher roles; are stated so as to make possible assessment of a student's behavior; and [are] made public in advance.
2. Criteria to be employed in assessing competencies are based upon specified competencies, . . . are explicit in setting levels of mastery under specified conditions, and [are] made public in advance.
3. Assessments of the student's competency uses his performance as the primary source of evidence; takes into account evidence of the student's

knowledge relevant to planning for, analyzing, interpreting, or evaluating situations or behaviors; and strives for objectivity.

4. The student's rate of progress through the program is determined by demonstrated competency rather than by time or course completion.

5. The instructional program is intended to facilitate the development and evaluation of the student's achievement of the competencies specified.

(With remarkable prescience, competency-based teacher education also was called "performance-based" teacher education. The two conceptions were considered identical.)

The preceding definition prompts some observations. While urging teacher educators to adopt competency-based programs, the committee also recommended a full-scale research effort to investigate the relationships between teacher competencies and the attainment of school objectives. In effect, little was known in 1971 about how competencies might link to school attainments. Note that condition 1 of the definition did not mandate that competencies be linked to school attainments in an empirical way, only that they be derived from explicit conceptions of teacher roles. So, although much of the rhetoric was that of "hard-headed" decision making, the process of determining the competencies to be included in a program was in fact quite arbitrary. Inspection of the *Reader's Guide to the Comprehensive Models for Preparing Elementary Teachers* (U.S. Office of Education, 1969) reveals, for example, that the competencies at Teachers College, Columbia University, were quite different from those at Michigan State University.

Also, note how condition 2 mimics the elements of behavioral objectives as advocated by Mager (1962) and Popham (1969), popular authors of the time.

The committee recommended a test of the power of competency-based teacher education to improve the performance of education personnel in the nation's schools (p. 24). The idea that the concept was more hypothesis than "manifest truth" was refreshing. We did not find this sentiment in any other reports that we reviewed for this book, nor in the reports with which the profession is currently dealing. The recommendations called for a committee for program planning and coordination; instructional laboratories for educational personnel; instructional materials for concept and skill attainment; instruments to define competencies in actual classrooms settings; and career development for master-level teachers and teacher trainers.

It is important to place the competency-based movement in context. The nation had largely rejected many of the major social and educational ideas popular in the 1960s, in particular, (1) open education based on the models of the British infant schools (popular in the education literature, although survey research at the time found that the ideas were not widely adopted); and (2) discipline-based education and teacher education, expressed in a large number of alphabet-soup projects—UICSM (University of Illinois Committee on School Mathematics), PSSC (Physical Sciences Study Committee), SMSG (School Mathematics Study Group), BSCS (Biological Sciences Curriculum Study), and scores of others. With the election of Richard M. Nixon in 1968 and a public backlash seeking the "basics" in education, the competency-based movement was launched in schools. Behavioral objectives were in, and the alphabet-soup programs, for the most part, were out.

The behavioral-objective advocates advanced a simple logic. No one could know how to plan a program if the objectives were not clear. Often the analogy of a ship's captain was used to clinch a debate: "How can a ship's captain know where to sail if he doesn't have a destination?" This persuasive argument, which turned Deweyian philosophy on its head, seemed convincing. The advocates were disappointed with the resistance that they saw in public schools. Some were quite aware that the behavioral-objective movement had a history in the "industrial efficiency" movements of the 1920s. They were convinced that, in a brief time, teachers would realize the cogency of their argument and adopt behavioral objectives. That did not happen.

In Texas, advocates of competency-based approaches went to the legislature to lobby for state laws mandating behavioral objectives for teacher education. The bill passed one of the houses. When it reached the other house, some legislators thought the idea so good that they broadened the mandate to include all courses and programs in higher education, not just teacher education. The resulting law required that all professors at Texas universities write behavioral objectives and use a competency-based approach. Eventually Texas courts blocked this effort, ruling that the legislation contravened state charters held by the universities, empowering faculty to make curriculum decisions.

What were the problems with competency-based teacher education? One was the difficulty in defining competencies. Fair-minded teacher educators could agree that all candidates should have the competency to plan a lesson, but they could not agree whether the competency should reflect Tyler's model, Gagné's model, or Taba's model. In other words, there was wide acceptance of the criteria, but considerable disagreement on the standards.

A second problem was the conceptual size of a proposed competency. Each competency advanced for consideration seemed to call for subcompetencies, which in turn called for sub-subcompetencies. The Michigan State model included about 1,500 such statements. In Stake's (1970) view, a wry observation made by E. Hersog in the late 1950s about efforts to write precise standards, applied in this circumstance:

> Big criteria have little criteria upon their backs to bite 'em.
> The small ones have still smaller, and so on *ad infinitum*. (p. 196)

On the one hand, the sheer number of competencies and the need to have assessment tasks for each of them made implementation and administration virtually impossible. On the other hand, the scope of the competencies and the detail of their attainment made one feel that successful candidates, if there were any, deserved a doctorate, not a bachelor's degree.

Finally, linking any specific, narrow competency to school attainments was difficult—and the logic of the movement fell on its own high-flown rhetoric.

A Nation Prepared: Teachers for the 21st Century, 1986

In 1986 the Carnegie Forum on Education and the Economy issued *A Nation Prepared: Teachers for the 21st Century*, the report of its Task Force on Teaching as a Profession. The Carnegie Forum was established in 1985 to draw the nation's attention to the link between economic growth and the skills and abilities of citizens. The mid-1980s was a boom time in some respects, but the nation faced economic problems, and the nation's leaders were uneasy about the ability of the United States to prosper in an era of global competition.

The report stated its theme thus:

> If our standard of living is to be maintained, if the growth of a permanent underclass is to be averted, if a democracy is to function effectively into the next century, our schools must graduate the vast majority of their students with achievement levels long thought possible for only the privileged few. (p. 3)

The report's recommendations for reinventing teacher education were less standards than mandates. They included the following:

1. All undergraduate degrees in education should be abolished by the states, and teacher education should become a graduate

enterprise. (This recommendation is an example of some apparent confusion at the time that continues to the present. States don't decide what degrees colleges and universities may offer; the governing boards of higher education institutions do. Of course, states can elect to approve or not to approve teacher education programs.)

2. Admission into teacher education programs should be contingent on applicants' mastery of basic skills and knowledge expected of all college graduates.

3. Graduate programs should allow candidates to make up course work missed in undergraduate programs during their graduate training.

4. States and others should offer incentives to attend graduate teacher education programs to students of exceptional academic ability and to qualified minority candidates.

5. A National Board for Professional Teaching Standards (NBPTS) should be created to establish standards for high levels of professional teaching competence and to issue certificates to people meeting those standards.

6. State and local policy should encourage higher education institutions and other providers to develop programs of continuing education to keep teachers abreast of the field and to prepare teachers for meeting the NBPTS standards.

The Carnegie Foundation itself acted on at least one of the recommendations of this report by funding (with others, including the federal government) NBPTS. In the ensuing years, NBPTS has awarded national certification to a significant number of teachers. In addition, much research and development has taken place on teacher evaluation, performance tests, setting of "cut scores," and other measurement applications that have generalizability throughout the field of teacher evaluation.

National Council for Accreditation of Teacher Education, 1952–

The effort to initiate national accreditation in teacher education has a long history. The normal schools organized themselves into a professional organization in the mid-1850s and struggled with the standards problem, but there was little interest in accreditation at that time (Haberman & Stinnett, 1973). Over time the American Normal School Association became a department of the NEA (1870), then metamorphosed into AATC (1917) and later AACTE (1948).

When regional associations refused to accredit normal schools because they were not mainstream colleges, teacher educators acting through AATC developed standards and began to accredit themselves, largely through self-study. This arrangement was considered suspect because governance of it was not sufficiently broad. In 1952 the TEPS Commission brought together other stakeholders, including AACTE, the National Association of State Directors of Teacher Education and Certification, and the Council of Chief State School Officers, to form NCATE. The original executive board included practitioners, teacher educators, representatives of state education authorities, and representatives of the National School Boards Association.

In the 1970s the organized profession became more prominent in the governance of NCATE, partially through the teacher empowerment movement that swept the country. The power of teacher organizations was increasing as they became more militant in the face of cutbacks in school budgets and salaries. Their zeal carried over into getting more deeply involved in state-level program-approval processes in teacher education. NEA issued a policy directive to all its state affiliates, urging them to lobby for autonomous professional standards boards, early field experiences, linkages with the field, shared governance of programs, and similar improvements. Although the reactions of state legislatures to the NEA agenda was varied, by the mid-1970s a handful of states had established professional standards boards, some autonomous, some not. (As of 1998, there was some form of standards board in 15 states.) Most wrote standards and developed program-approval policies and procedures that introduced new challenges to teacher educators. Where state legislatures legally sanctioned such boards, these evaluation processes were high-stake efforts because if the standards board did not approve an institution's program, for all intents and purposes, teacher education at that institution was out of business.

In this context, NCATE floundered. Earning national accreditation was of no consequence, and neither was not earning it. Faculties asked their deans, "Why are we doing NCATE?" The NCATE report seemed to be similar to the state report, but there was no mechanism to have one substitute for the other. States and NCATE each guarded their precious perquisites.

Prodded by exigencies that virtually threatened its continued existence, NCATE entered into a "redesign phase." Working cooperatively,

NEA and AACTE representatives elected to forgo accrediting teacher education programs because the states were doing that, and to accredit institutional "units" instead. Some observers saw this distinction as an effort to play down the charge that the NCATE and state approval processes were redundant. The concept in effect called on units (schools, colleges, and departments of education) to be responsible for ensuring that all professional teacher education programs on campus met NCATE standards. The standards were written at the unit level, not the program level. They reflected many of the recommendations identified earlier: rigorous standards of admission, high standards for faculty, specified student teaching, shared governance of teacher education, and more. They were organized into four categories: design of professional education; candidates in professional education; professional education faculty; and the unit for professional education.

There also were at least two new concerns: (1) diversity of student body and faculty and (2) a conceptual frame. The diversity indicators associated with NCATE standards included the following (NCATE, 1995):

II.B.1: The unit has and implements an explicit plan with adequate resources to recruit, admit, and retain a diverse student body.

II.B.3: The student body is culturally diverse.

III.B.1: The unit has and implements an explicit plan with adequate resources to ensure hiring and retaining of a diverse faculty.

The standard for a conceptual frame was based on the notion that in 1986 there was new knowledge to guide teacher education programming and planning. The irony that such an insight also motivated the 1870 reports evidently was lost on the profession. Forgoing the familiar name "curriculum standard," the authors of the redesign, with some conceit, called the new standard the "knowledge base standard."

The standard called on the unit to advance a point of view about teaching that was widely accepted by faculty and associated public school personnel. (It is interesting to wonder if all the professors at the Harvard Law School have similar conceptions of justice and the legal profession.) In a sense the conceptual frame answered the question, "What sort of teacher are you working to develop in your program?" Some institutions advanced one answer for all the programs in its unit, whereas others developed separate frames for each program. The problem with doing the latter was that candidates in various programs might share core courses or foundations courses. If one program was Skinnerian in its conceptual frame and another essentially Piagetian, the instruction in the shared courses might become schizophrenic. But this new standard was seen as highly innovative. Actually most of the institutions that subsequently failed to achieve NCATE accreditation on the initial visit failed this standard more than they failed the others.

It also is instructive to consider what standards NCATE did not adopt in the redesign period. As Haberman and Stinnett (1973) note, one of the original and enduring motives for having national accreditation was to shut down the diploma mills in teacher education. Traditionalists worried about well-funded efforts, such as Nova University (our example, not Haberman and Stinnett's), offering teacher education programs in various states out of a shell in one state.

Lynn Gubser, then executive director of NCATE, proposed a criterion based on economic support of programs, setting a rather steep standard for, in effect, how much budget should stand behind every teacher education candidate. This motion received little support within AACTE.

Another proposal, advanced with similar motivation, called for each program to have a critical mass of faculty, roughly defined as "more than four." The idea was that schools of education should not offer, for example, a science education program or an educational administration program, with one professor. This motion also lost.

Finally, the new NCATE standards took "context" into consideration. This challenged teacher educators' commitment to their own standards. For example, the teacher education community supports the diversity standards of NCATE. Observers can presume that faculty and student diversity is important for candidates who are going to be licensed to teach in the public schools of the country. But members of the NCATE Board of Examiners are instructed to take context into account when applying these standards. If the members are visiting a Catholic college in the remote middle west, miles from an urban center, the standards are less important than if the members are applying them to an urban university. The rationale for this differentiation is not well understood, but the differentiation calls to mind the warnings of the 1870s, cited earlier, that standards should not be overly ambitious.

Restructuring the Education of Teachers, 1991

In 1991 the Association of Teacher Educators' Commission on the Education of Teachers into the 21st Century published a set of recommendations that grew from "an intensive 18-month examination of the complex factors that influence the quality of teacher education" (p. v). At 10 open hearings across the country, the commission made proposals for action, and nearly 70 well-informed teacher educators in about 30 states analyzed and commented on drafts of the report.

The report began with a candid rundown of then-current circumstances in education and teacher education, then sketched a hoped-for future in the 1990s and the 21st century. It outlined conditions in society and education that influence teaching and schooling. Also, it cited mandates and other steps to advance teacher education. The commission stated a preference for "state-level policy" that focuses on "inducements and capacity building to enhance performance," over policy that mandates compliance (p. 5). Recommendations "address[ed] all phases and aspects of teacher education: recruitment and selection, preservice preparation, entry into teaching, continuing professional development, and needed research and accountability" (p. 6).

The commission expressed concern about the numerous steps "taken to advance teacher education" that had not yielded major improvements. It recognized limited efforts, resistance to change, underfunding, and "lack of a *collective* will to act" as barriers to advocated actions (p. 5). The commission offered a series of recommendations, specifying for each one the needed actions by teacher educators in colleges, schools, state agencies, and national, state, and local professional organizations.

The report gave special emphasis to preparing teachers to teach children and youth who were at risk, minority, and poor, particularly those in urban areas. The commission expressed disquiet about the existing teaching force—mainly white, English speaking, and (in schools) primarily female—which would be expected to teach an increasingly diverse population of students. The commission advocated recruitment and preparation of teachers who were not culture bound, who had skills and attitudes to deal effectively with a diversity of students.

The commission complained that most recommendations for reform had come from national commissions outside teacher education. It exhorted those *within* teacher education to establish priorities for improving teacher education: "What is needed is an agenda that specifies different responsibilities for appropriate individuals and groups and calls for action within realistic timelines" (p. 5). The commission recommended "an interrelated set of policies and positions to improve the education of teachers . . . that can be adopted immediately, then monitored and evaluated" (p. 5).

Questions Basic to Standards

In considering the strategy of writing standards for teacher education, or for any educational process, from standards for professional development schools to standards for mathematics teaching, we think that several questions are pertinent:

- Over time, what have been the motivations or the reasons for setting standards?
- To what extent have the content and the process of standards changed?
- What changes in teacher education over the last 130 years have resulted from various standards efforts?
- What factors have detracted from applying standards?

Over time, what have been the motivations or the reasons for setting standards?

Throughout history, one motivation for advocating standards has been the extent of diversity among teacher education programs. Some observers have asserted that variety, at least to the extent that it is present in teacher education, must include weak programs, and weak programs should be eliminated. Leaders in teacher education have hoped for development of consensus concerning the tough questions, such as "What is a good teacher?" and "What must good teachers know and be able to do?" It has seemed at times more important to have agreement than to "get it right."

A second motivation has been economic. As the U.S. economy has faced parlous times, with grim forecasts for the future, some have argued that weak students are partially responsible for the economic decline. In some respects the schools have been treated as scapegoats.

Recently, another motivation was alarm at the results of international testing. Students in the United States were reported to be doing poorly compared with students in Germany, Japan, and Korea. At the time the economies of those nations were booming, and the apparent correlation between high scores on the international tests and national prosperity seemed compelling. With the economies of Germany, Japan, and Korea now in recession, the link seems more problematic.

To what extent have the content and the process of standards changed?
Over time, standards have been fairly consistent, changing mainly when the process of teacher education has been altered. For example:

1. When student teaching took place in laboratory schools, teachers in those schools supervised it. As student teaching began occurring in public schools, it became a shared function of college supervisors and cooperating teachers.

2. When teacher education was assessed on process and resources, state approval and national accreditation evaluated the conditions of preparation—faculty, facilities, library and other resources, curriculum content, and student teaching and other laboratory experiences. As priorities changed and teacher education became more product oriented, evaluation focused on outcomes and performance of graduates.

What changes in teacher education over the last 130 years have resulted from various standards efforts?
This brief history has documented 130 years' worth of efforts to set standards for teacher education. We can cite the following changes:

1. Preparation is now universally four years in length for both elementary and secondary school teachers.

2. Pre-student-teaching clinical experiences have become more focused, more numerous, and better organized.

3. Student teaching has moved from limited experiences in laboratory schools to full-time multiweek assignments in real settings (public schools).

4. Student teaching sometimes includes two or more assignments—in different schools, at different levels, with different types of students.

5. Supervision of student teaching often is done by cooperating teachers with some training in guiding neophytes. College and university supervision vacillates from the use of highly qualified professors to the use of sometimes poorly qualified graduate assistants.

6. Numerous universities bring selected teachers to the college as clinical instructors for one- or two-year assignments.

7. New role designations have been created for "site-based teacher educators," teachers specially trained to participate in

guiding clinical experiences, supervising student teaching and other clinical experiences, and mentoring beginning teachers.

8. Methods courses have become more reality based, often team-taught by professors and practicing teachers, sometimes in a school setting.

9. Some programs group prospective teachers in cohorts. This provides more continuity in preparation, fosters team building, and offers experience in working together.

10. E-mail has enhanced communication between professors and prospective teachers about course work and clinical experiences.

11. Portfolios are used to record the growth and the progress of prospective teachers.

There have been many changes, but often it is not clear whether they are improvements. For example, the commonsense notion that more time in schools before student teaching will improve preparation has been widely adopted but not evaluated. The costs of mounting such programs in terms of weakening the arts and science components of teacher education programs, and the escalating costs of teacher education because of these additional clinical requirements, have not been assessed against the gain that candidates were expected to achieve.

Why have there not been more serious efforts to evaluate changes? One answer is lack of a credible criterion. What evidence would count as supporting an intervention? Another answer is multiple-treatment interference in any evaluation design. Often, teacher educators do not make just one change in a program—they make many. The effects of early field experiences, additional special education courses, new emphases on multicultural education, and other innovations interact, making evaluation extremely difficult. Most changes reflect common sense on the part of teacher boards or national panels of experts. No one has data.

What factors have detracted from applying standards?

Smith (1980) identified a central factor detracting from the application of standards: the authority and the traditions of the college and university settings in which most teacher education programs are embedded. For purposes of "reputation" and "image," teacher education has embraced the university as the proper home of professional studies. But, unlike the professions of law and medicine, teacher education has been unable to escape campus regulations and customs governed by faculty senates. Further, professors hired into teacher education programs at universities have taken their cues for promotion, tenure, and success from arts and science colleagues. They have resisted field assignments such as supervising student teachers, instead hiring graduate students, junior faculty, and adjunct faculty to do those jobs. They also have resisted advising undergraduates. Smith argued that teacher education had to free itself from the shackles of higher education with the aid of state government and state policy.

Another factor is that people disagree with some of the recommended standards. For almost every recommendation, there is a sensible counterargument. Take the idea of making teacher education a graduate program. People argue earnestly that when education is trying to attract more minorities into teaching, making teacher education more elitist goes in the wrong direction. Further, the cost of a teaching certificate would be high (not counting deferred income), and beginning salaries seldom go higher than $25,000. Economically it doesn't make sense. Equally cogent arguments can be made about higher admission standards, early clinical experience, extended student teaching, shared governance on university committees, state-mandated tests for licensure, and so on.

A third factor is that discerning differences in graduates' behavior once they are in the classroom is difficult. The powerful socialization of the workplace, documented by Lortie (1975) and Rosenholtz (1989), washes out training effects. This influence is present in nursing and medicine as well. So the introduction of innovations on the campus is difficult to justify empirically.

Fourth, teacher education is a low priority on campus. Many of the recommendations require enormous increases in education budgets—to fund professional development schools, to pay for supervision of early clinical experiences, to add advisers and counselors, and the like. If a provost had money to spend, one of the last places he or she would spend it would be on these add-ons. And there is little evidence that these improvements make candidates better teachers or more attractive in the marketplace.

Standards also have suffered from the profession's lack of ability to communicate with the public and with policy makers. The profession has not conveyed the importance of education, it has not informed the citizenry about the real needs of education, and it has failed to secure adequate support. Education has never been packaged as effectively as news or science. There are no Jim Lehrers, Carl Sagans, Joan Ganz Cooneys, or National Geographic Societies purveying education. The profession has not made learning appealing, attractive, and stimulating in the minds of laypeople. No one thinks much about, or spends considerable money on, developing standards for informing people about education. Thus public opinion does not demand greater support for education, and state legislators regularly get reelected without funding education or teacher education adequately. The resources required to produce quality education are comparable to those going into the production of television programs or distance learning. The public and policy makers have never recognized that fact.

Another deterrent to the application of standards is the inadequacy of information on supply and demand of teachers. Anticipating shortages and surpluses is very complicated. With no tracking system on the availability of qualified teachers, standards for teacher licensure are determined more by the supply of personnel than by the quality of personnel. Standards rise and fall depending on supply and demand.

Still another factor hindering the application of standards is the gap between the cultures of school and university faculties. The differences in the work lives, prestige, personal and academic freedom, professional climates, and financial rewards are greater than in almost any other profession. Most professors of education have been teachers, but few would return to schoolteaching.

Finally, the vastness of the profession is a constant dilemma. There are more than 2.5 million teachers in the United States. Teacher education programs are among the largest on university campuses. Fifty state jurisdictions set standards for program approval and licensure. So changing an education or certification requirement for teachers—for instance, introducing a course on conflict management—is not only incredibly expensive but difficult and complicated to enforce.

Lessons Learned in the Last 130 Years

In an earlier section we sketch the results of major studies and projects that have recommended standards for teacher education. Our selection is a sample of many such efforts by thoughtful, highly competent educators, teacher educators, and others. The refrain of their conclusions has been so constant, no matter what the era, that something other than good thinking must be lacking. Is seeking standards too narrow a focus?

We have discerned four patterns:

1. The recommendations for improving teacher education are remarkably similar over 130 years: brighter students, more compe-

tent faculty, more realistic classes, rigorous general education, serious (performance) evaluation, collaborative planning, and so forth.

2. Raising of standards is motivated in part by (a) perceptions of dire national needs—for example, *A Nation at Risk* (National Commission on Excellence in Education, 1983) and *What Matters Most* (National Commission on Teaching & America's Future, 1996); (b) concerns with the variation in preparation programs—with variation there must be error, and error must be snuffed out; and (c) the availability of new science or knowledge to give direction where it was absent in the past.

3. Almost none of the reports we summarized acknowledged previous reports. Their efforts were almost totally ahistorical, with no authors wondering why the profession had either ignored previous recommendations or adopted them without changing dramatically the practice of teachers or the status of teaching.

4. Finally, although all the reports shared uncommon zeal for the standards they were promulgating, there was very little evidence in the reports or in the literature of the time to support the recommendations. Instead, the recommendations seemed to represent "self-evident" beliefs.

The drive over 130 years to set and apply standards in teacher education has yielded some results, but no major breakthroughs. Current attempts to examine and align standards will probably accomplish no more than prior efforts if deliberators do not address other considerations.

For example, the narrowness of most attempts to improve teaching and teacher education has limited the possibility of progress. Even the best programs can amount to naught when graduates are unable to practice in the real world of schools what they have learned in college. If reform in education is to be achieved, creating and monitoring standards on the conditions of work in schools is imperative.

The teaching profession's power is so fragmented, and its prestige so ailing, that adequate emphasis on and sufficient financial support for teacher education, professional practice, and continuing professional development are dim prospects. A coalition of organizations could become a professional political force that could generate support to achieve a major breakthrough in the quality of schooling and teacher education. This would mean cooperation between the practicing and the preparing arms of the profession. It would mean organizations and agencies working together and compromising on vested interests. A coalition with such a base and such agreement would be difficult to hold back in the society.

The irony is that the people of the United States have achieved great progress primarily because of the educational level of the population, yet education is not well regarded and supported.

References

American Council on Education, Commission on Teacher Education. (1946). *The improvement of teacher education.* Washington, DC: American Council on Education.

American Normal School Association. (1869). Proceedings of the Fifth Annual Meeting, August 17, 1869, Trenton, NJ. In *Proceedings of the NEA National Meeting.* Washington, DC: National Education Association.

American Normal School Association. (1870). Proceedings of the Sixth Annual Meeting. In *Journal of Proceedings and Addresses of the National Meeting of the NEA.* Washington, DC: National Education Association.

Association of Teacher Educators. (1991). *Restructuring the education of teachers* (Report of the Commission on the Education of Teachers into the 21st Century). Reston, VA: Author.

Carnegie Forum on Education and the Economy, Task Force on Teaching as a Profession. (1986). *A nation prepared: Teachers for the 21st century.* New York: Carnegie Forum on Education and the Economy.

Charters, W. W., & Waples, D. (1929). *The Commonwealth teacher-training study.* Chicago: University of Chicago Press.

Elam, S. (1971). *Performance-based teacher education: What is the state of the art?* Washington, DC: American Association of Colleges for Teacher Education.

Glass, G. (1978). Standards and criteria. *Journal of Educational Measurement, 15,* 237–62.

Haberman, M., & Stinnett, T. M. (1973). *Teacher education and the new profession of teaching.* Berkeley, CA: McCutchan.

Howsam, R. B., Corrigan, D. C., Denemark, G. W., & Nash, R. J. (1976/1985). *Educating a profession.* Washington, DC: American Association of Colleges for Teacher Education.

Lindsey, M. (Ed.). (1961). *New horizons for the teaching profession.* Washington, DC: National Education Association, National Commission on Teacher Education and Professional Standards.

Lortie, D. C. (1975). *School-teacher: A sociological study.* Chicago: University of Chicago Press.

Mager, R. F. (1962). *Preparing instructional objectives.* Palo Alto, CA: Fearon.

Mayor, J. (1965). *Accreditation in teacher education.* Washington, DC: National Committee on Accrediting.

National Commission on Excellence in Education. (1983). *A nation at risk: The imperative for educational reform.* Washington, DC: Author.

National Commission on Teaching & America's Future. (1996). *What matters most: Teaching for America's future.* New York: Columbia University, Teachers College.

National Council for Accreditation of Teacher Education. (1995). *Standards, procedures, and policies for the accreditation of professional education units.* Washington, DC: Author.

National Education Association, Department of Normal Schools. (1899). Secretary's minutes. Report of the Committee on Normal Schools. In *Journal of Proceedings and Addresses of the 38th Annual Meeting of the NEA.* Washington, DC: National Education Association.

Pearson, P. D. (1994). Standards and teacher education: A policy perspective. In M. E. Diez, V. Richardson, & P. D. Pearson (Eds.), *Setting standards and educating teachers* (pp. 37–67). Washington, DC: American Association of Colleges for Teacher Education.

Popham, W. J. (1969). *Instructional objectives.* Chicago: Rand McNally.

Richardson, V. (1994). Standards and assessments: What is their educative potential? In M. E. Diez, V. Richardson, & P. D. Pearson (Eds.), *Setting standards and educating teachers* (pp. 15–36). Washington, DC: American Association of Colleges for Teacher Education.

Rosenholtz, S. J. (1989). *Teachers' workplace: The social organization of schools.* White Plains, NY: Longman.

Rosner, B. (1972). *The power of competency-based teacher education: Report of the Committee on National Program Priorities in Teacher Education.* Boston: Allyn and Bacon.

Smith, B. O. (1969). *Teachers for the real world.* Washington, DC: American Association of Colleges for Teacher Education.

Smith, B. O. (1980). *A design for a school of pedagogy.* Washington, DC: U.S. Department of Education.

Stake, R. E. (1970, April). Objectives, priorities, and other judgment data. *Review of Educational Research, 40,* 181–212.

Sub-Committee of the Standards and Surveys Committee of the American Association of Teachers Colleges. (1948). *School and community laboratory experiences in teacher education*. Oneonta, NY: American Association of Teachers Colleges.

U.S. Office of Education. (1969). *A reader's guide to the comprehensive models for preparing elementary teachers*. Washington, DC: Author. (ERIC Document Reproduction Service No. 034 076)

Other Reports

American Association of Colleges for Teacher Education. (1956). *Teacher education for a free people*. Washington, DC: Author.

American Council on Education, Commission on Teacher Education. (1944). *Teachers for our time*. Washington, DC: American Council on Education.

Conant, J. B. (1963). *The education of American teachers*. New York: McGraw–Hill.

Consortium for Excellence in Teacher Education. (1987). *Beginning dialogue*. Middlebury, VT: Author.

Consortium for Excellence in Teacher Education. (1987). *Teacher education and the liberal arts*. Swarthmore College, PA: Author.

Goodlad, J. I. (1990). *Teachers for our nation's schools*. San Francisco: Jossey–Bass.

Holmes Group. (1986). *Tomorrow's teachers*. East Lansing, MI: Author.

Holmes Group. (1995). *Tomorrow's schools of education*. East Lansing, MI: Author.

Interstate New Teacher Assessment and Support Consortium. (1992). *Model standards for beginning teacher licensing and development: A resource for state dialogue*. Washington, DC: Council of Chief State School Officers.

Kaplan, L., & Edelfelt, R. A. (Eds.). (1996). *Teachers for the new millennium: Aligning teacher development, national goals, and high standards for all students*. Thousand Oaks, CA: Corwin Press.

Murray, F. B., & Fallon, D. (1989). *The reform of teacher education for the 21st century* (Project 30 One-Year Report). Newark, DE: University of Delaware.

National Association of State Directors of Teacher Education and Certification. (1992). *Outcome-based standards and portfolio assessment*. Dubuque, IA: Kendall/Hunt.

National Commission for Excellence in Teacher Education. (1985). *A call for change in teacher education*. Washington, DC: American Association of Colleges for Teacher Education.

National Commission on Excellence in Education. (1983). *A nation at risk: The imperative for educational reform.* Washington, DC: Author.

National Commission on Teaching & America's Future. (1996). *What matters most: Teaching for America's future.* New York: Columbia University, Teachers College.

National Education Association. (1982). *Excellence in our schools. Teacher education: An action plan.* Washington, DC: Author.

Smith, B. O. (1969). *Teachers for the real world.* Washington, DC: American Association of Colleges for Teacher Education.

Southern Regional Education Board. (1986). Major reports on teacher education: What do they mean for states? *Regional Spotlight, 15*(1), 1–6.

Study Commission on Undergraduate Education and the Education of Teachers. (1976). *Teacher education in the United States: The responsibility gap.* Lincoln, NE: University of Nebraska Press.